I0468926

POWWOW COLORS

Vol. 1

ISBN-13: 978-1530654062
ISBN-10: 1530654068

On the way to the powwow, you can sometimes see the tops of the lodge poles before you get there.

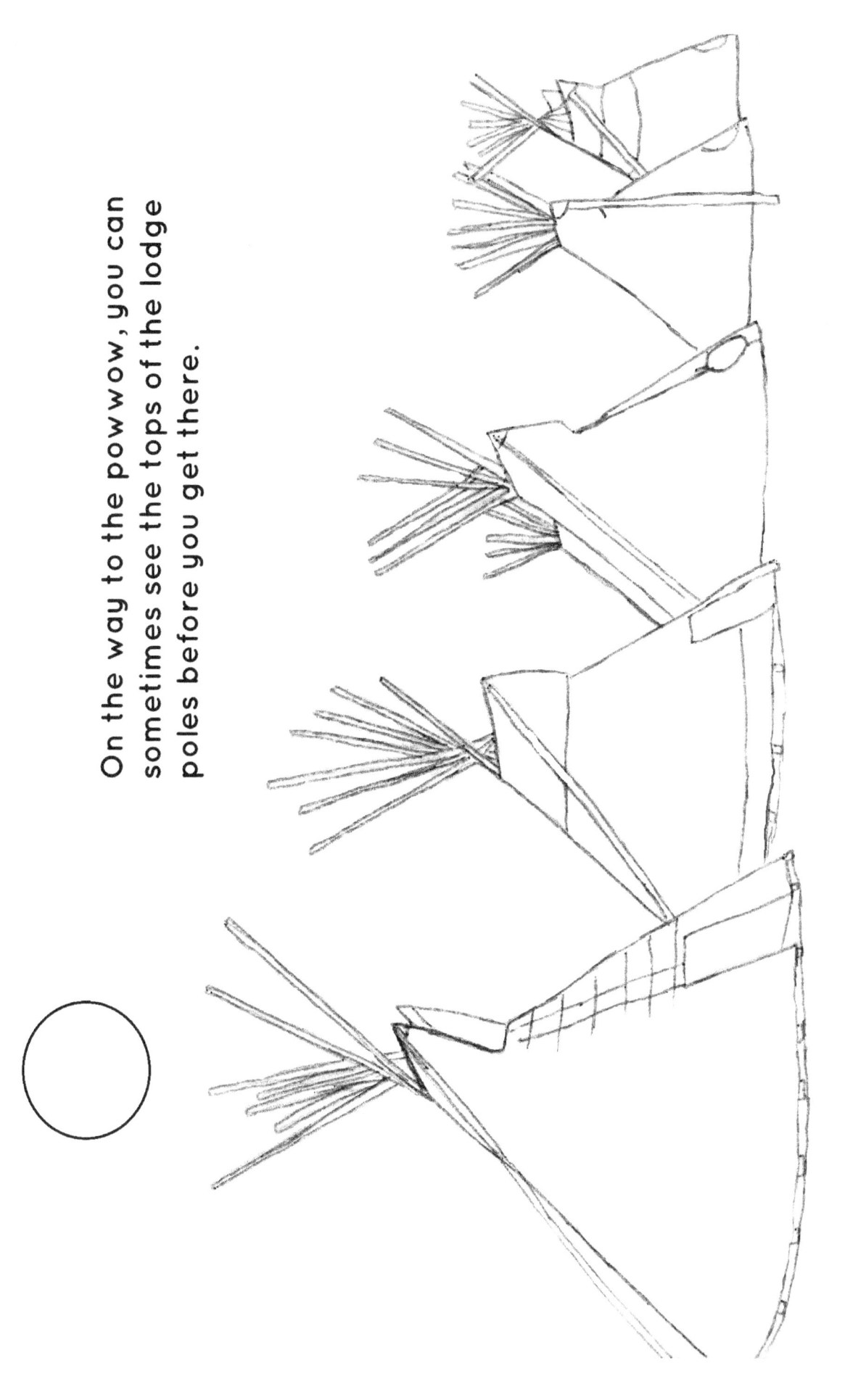

The busiest vendors are the Frybread trailers, that are sometimes painted bright colors.

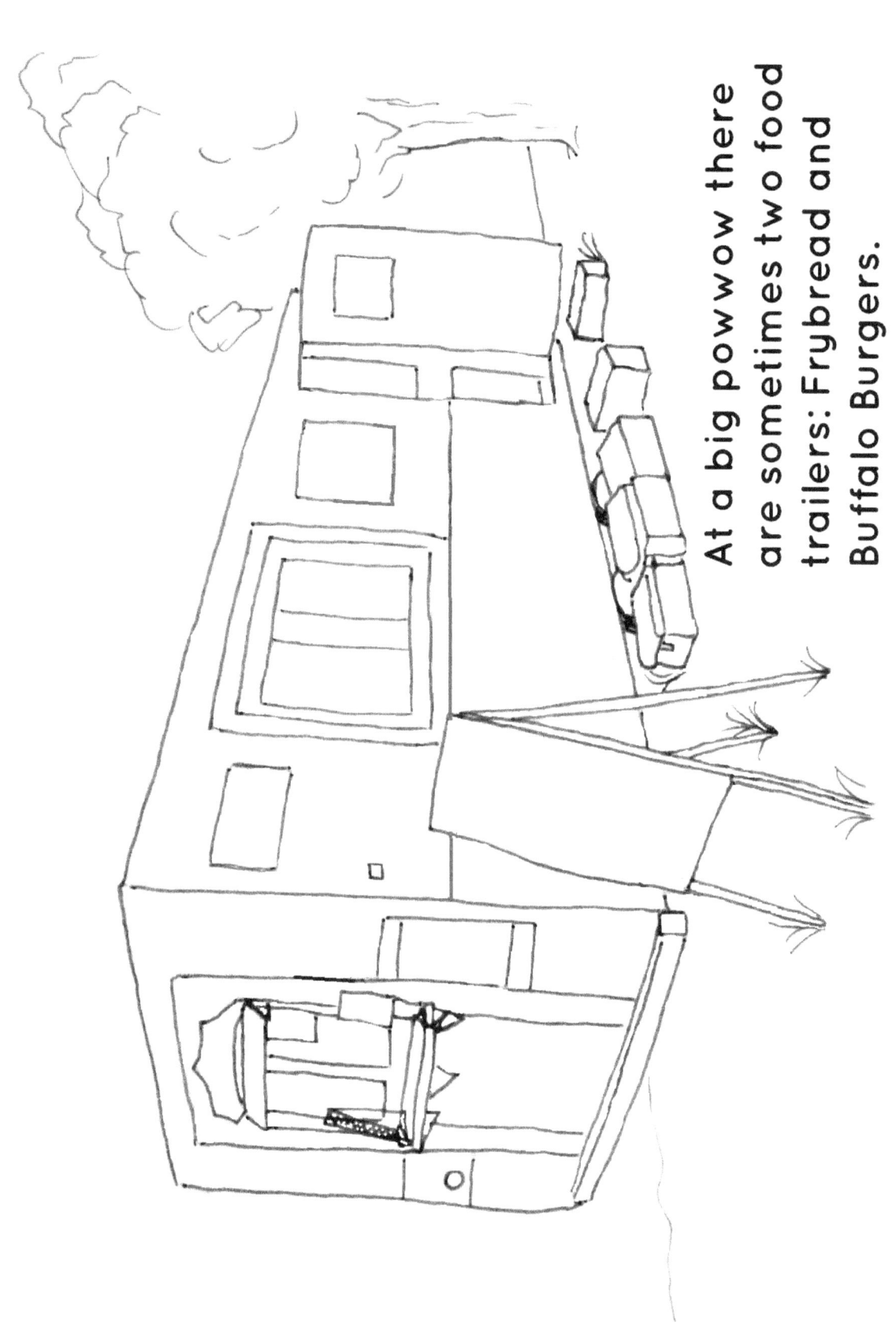

At a big powwow there are sometimes two food trailers: Frybread and Buffalo Burgers.

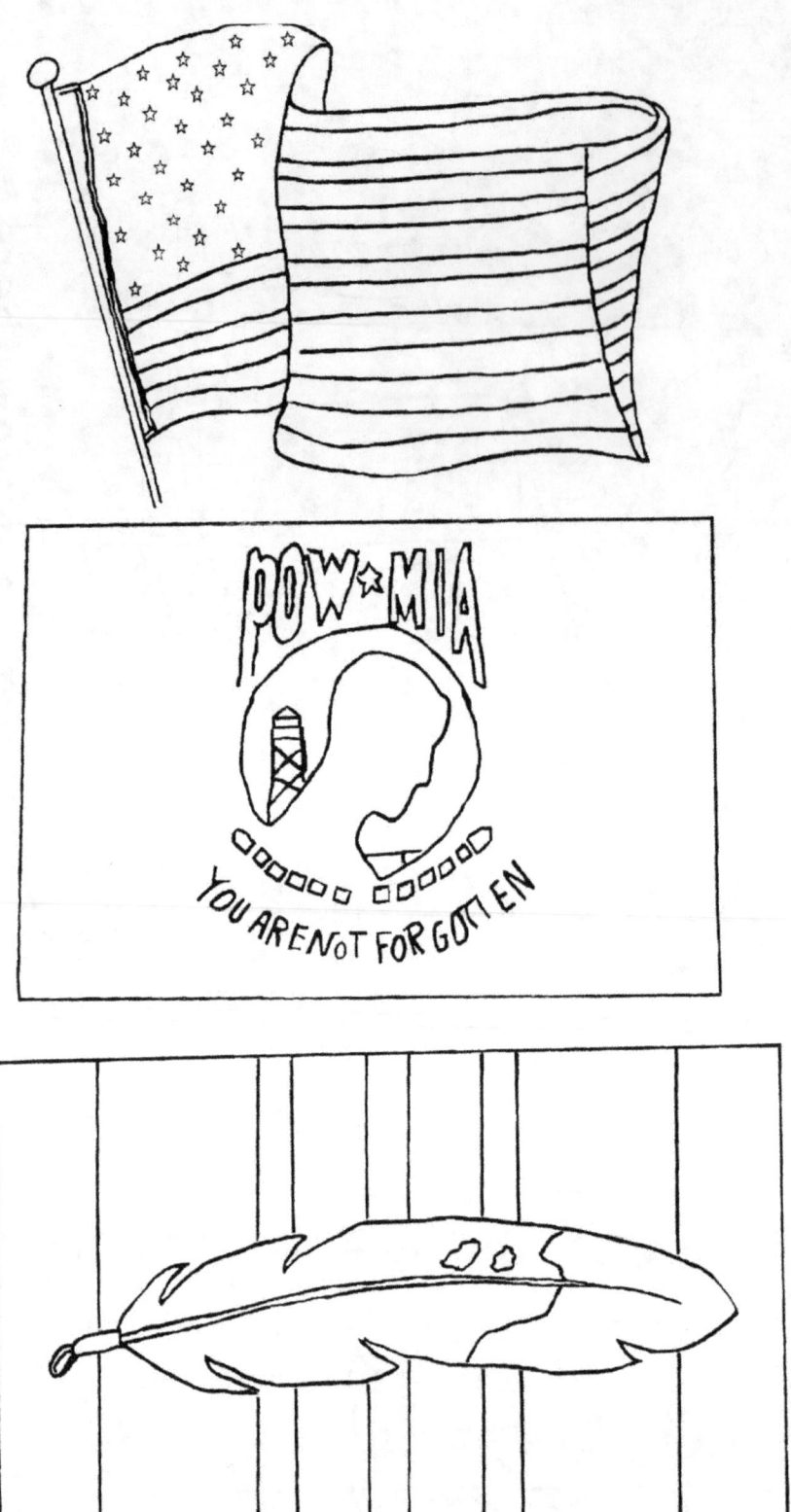

Flags hold an important place of respect in Native communities and at powwows they lead the dancers into the arbor.

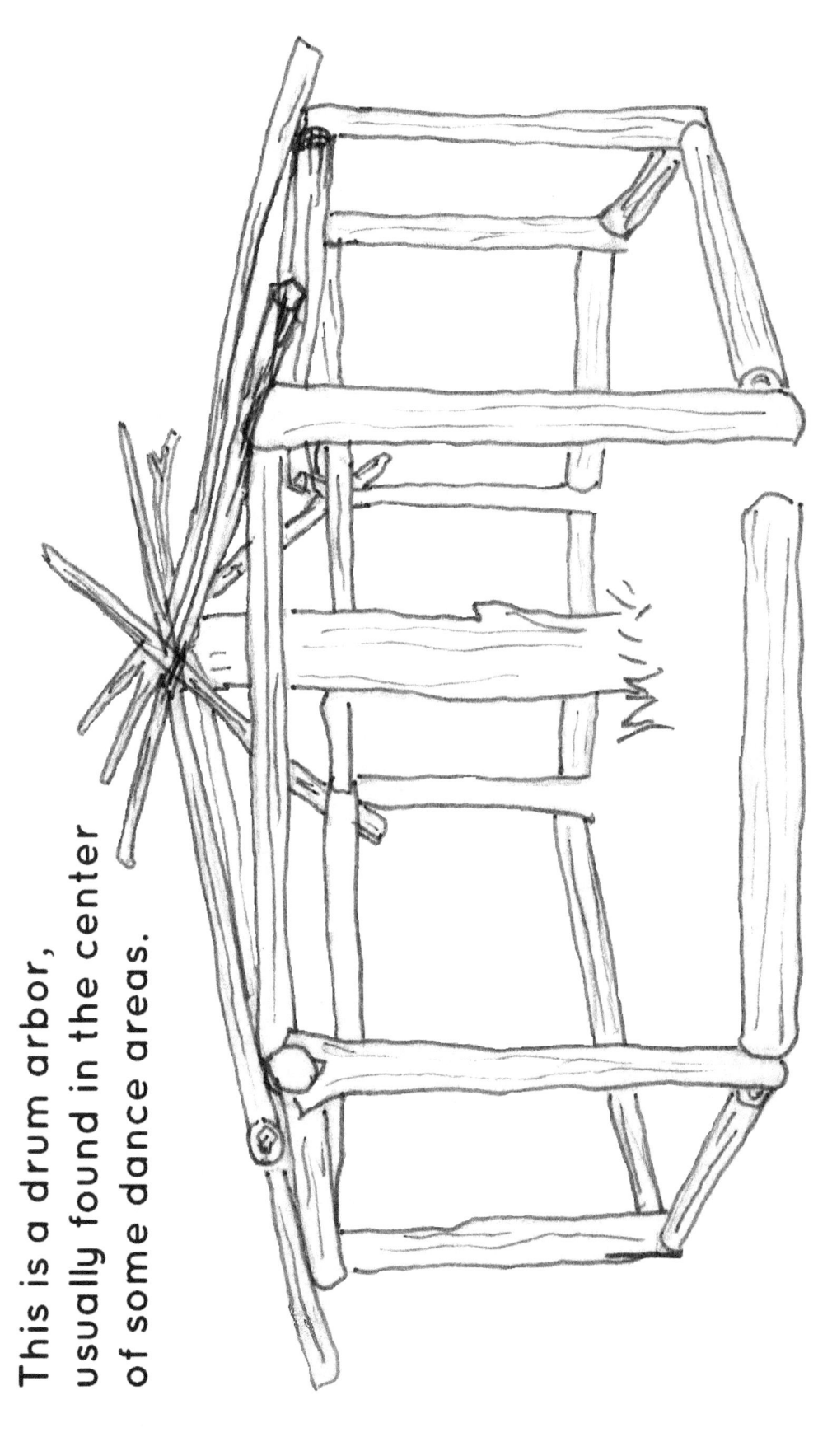

This is a drum arbor, usually found in the center of some dance areas.

Of the many drums, the big, loud drum is the heart beat of the people and the powwow. It starts the day and closes down the dance.

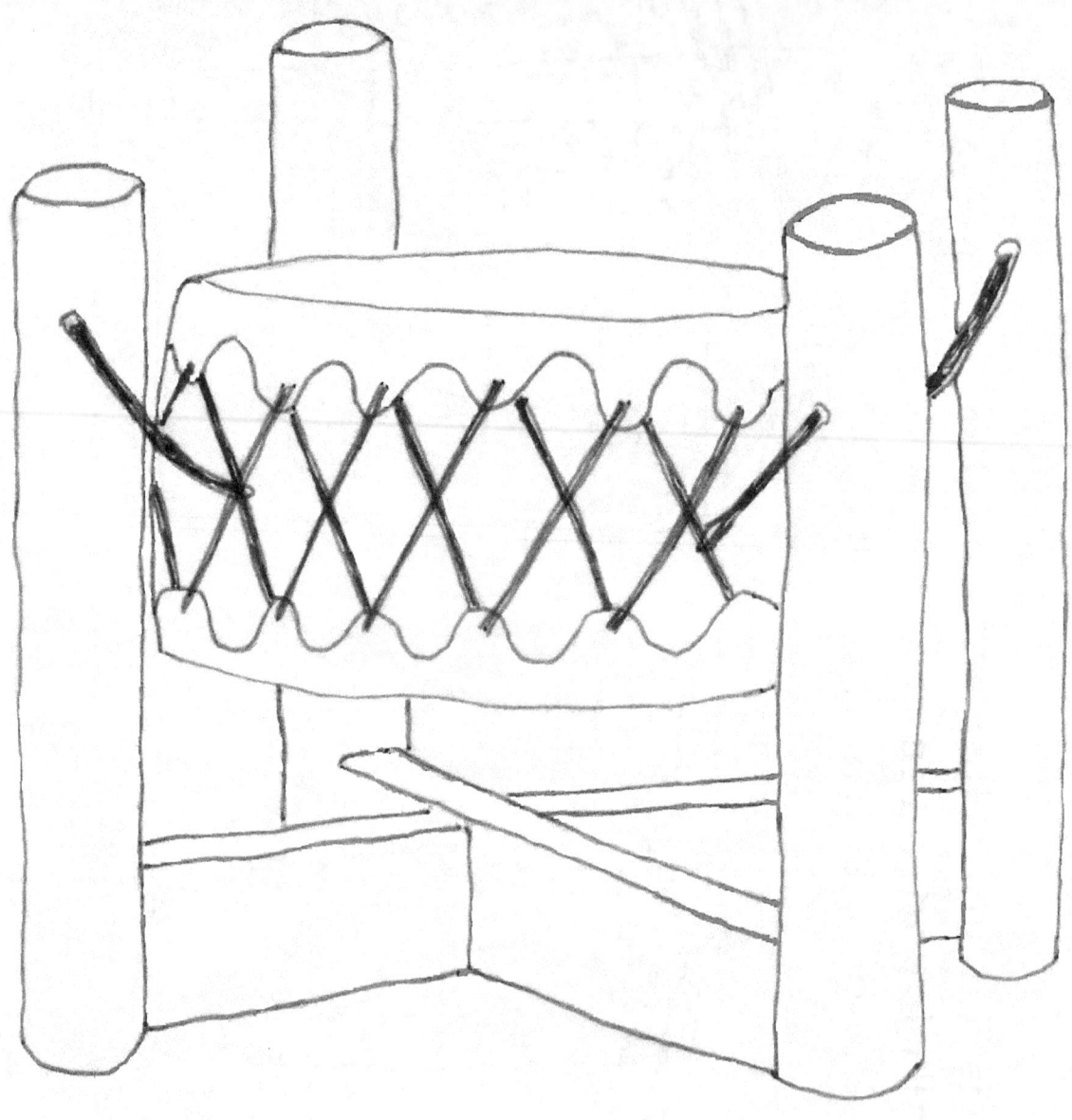

Feathers hold a special place in the lives of Native Peoples. All dancers wear feathers of some kind. These are Hawk, Owl and Eagle. Feathers should never be touched without permission.

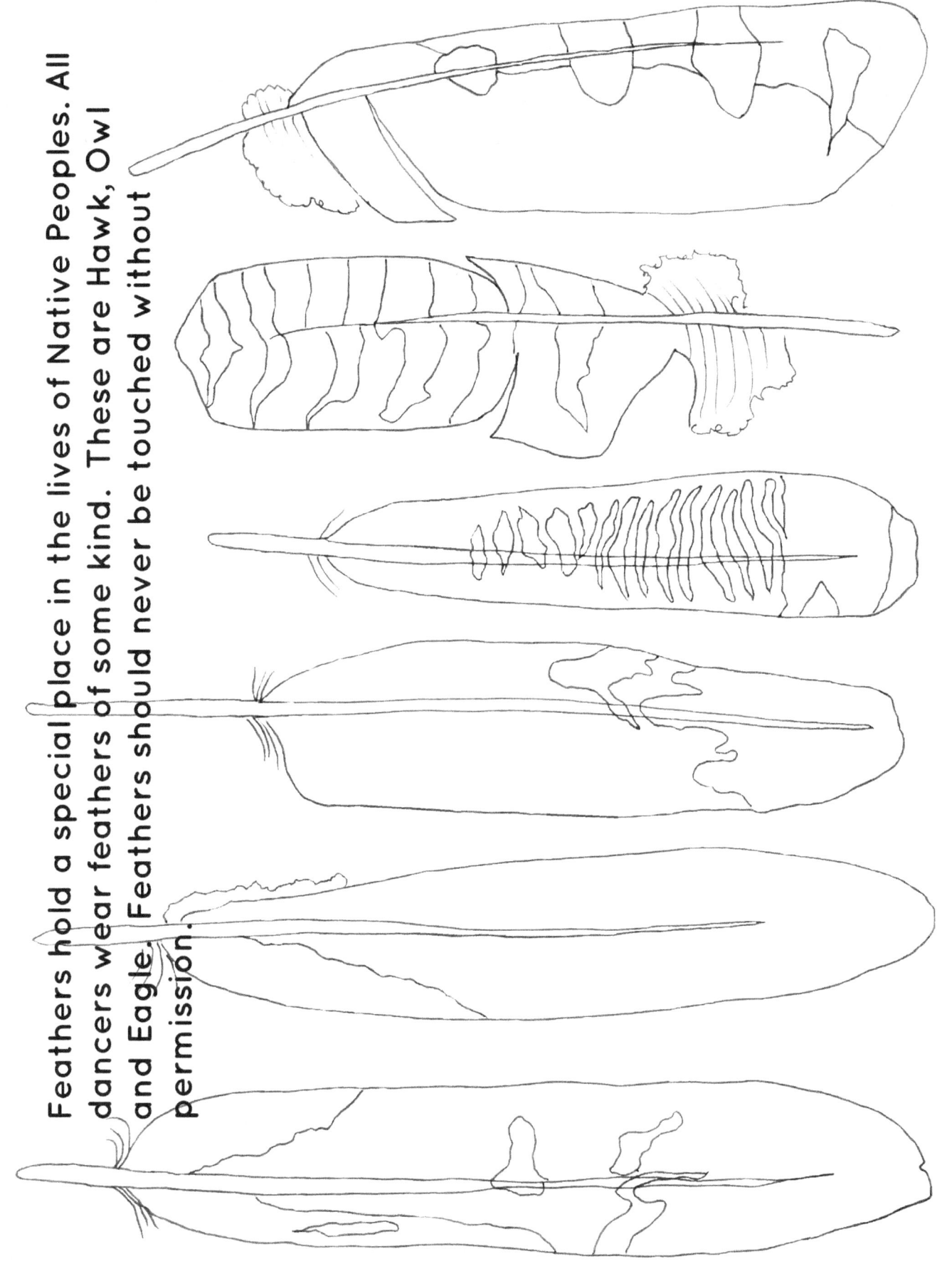

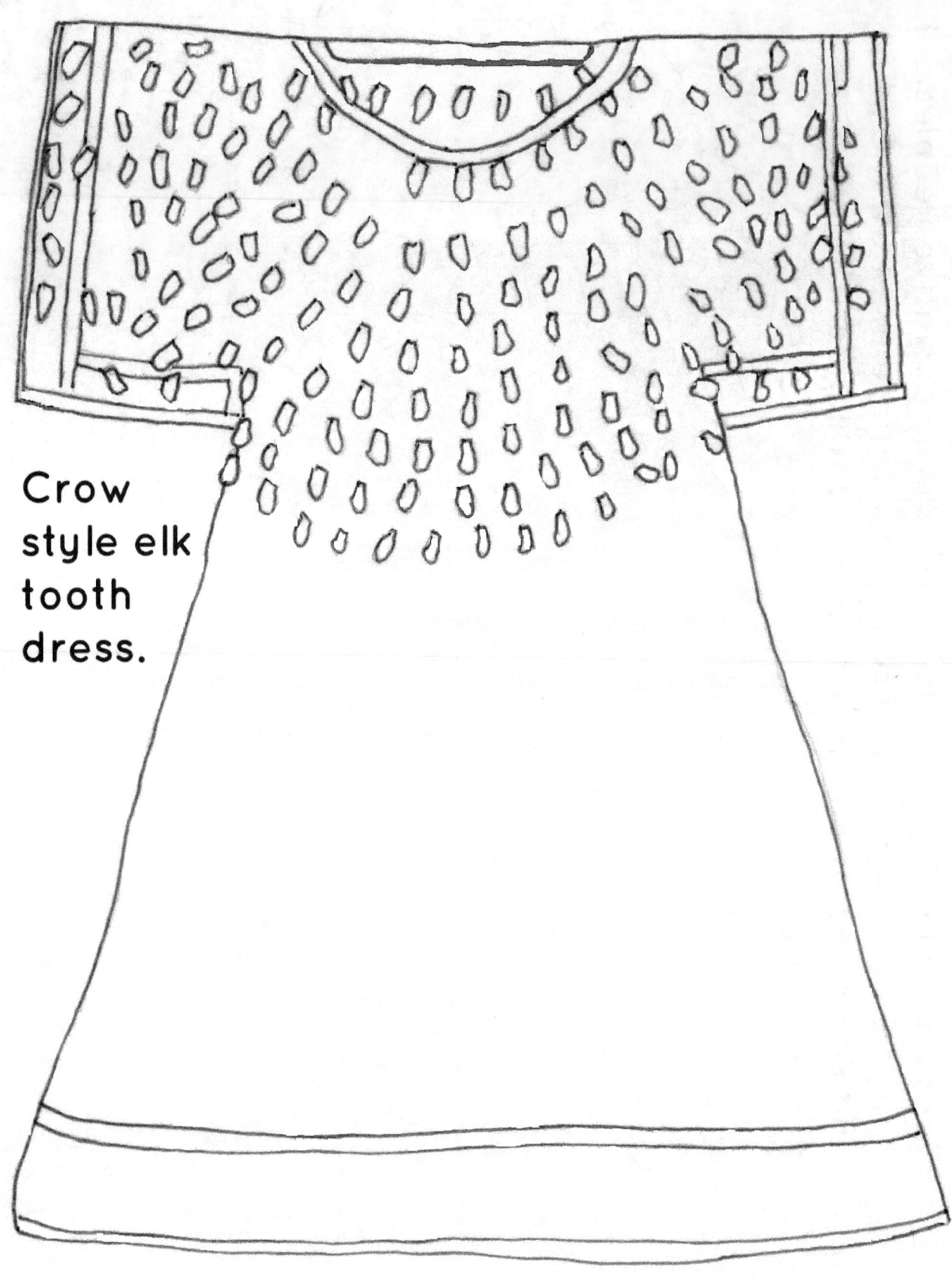

Crow
style elk
tooth
dress.

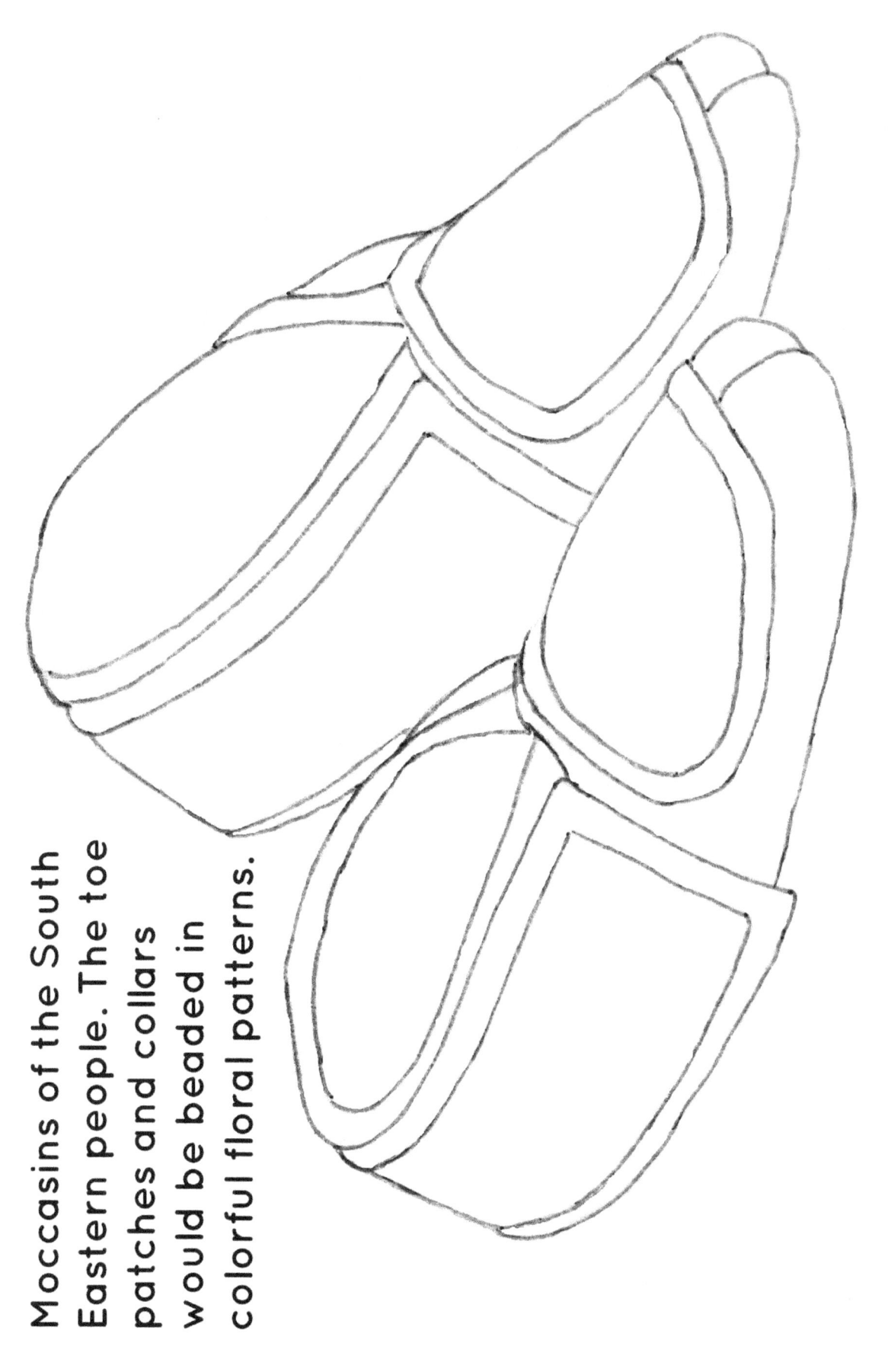

Moccasins of the South Eastern people. The toe patches and collars would be beaded in colorful floral patterns.

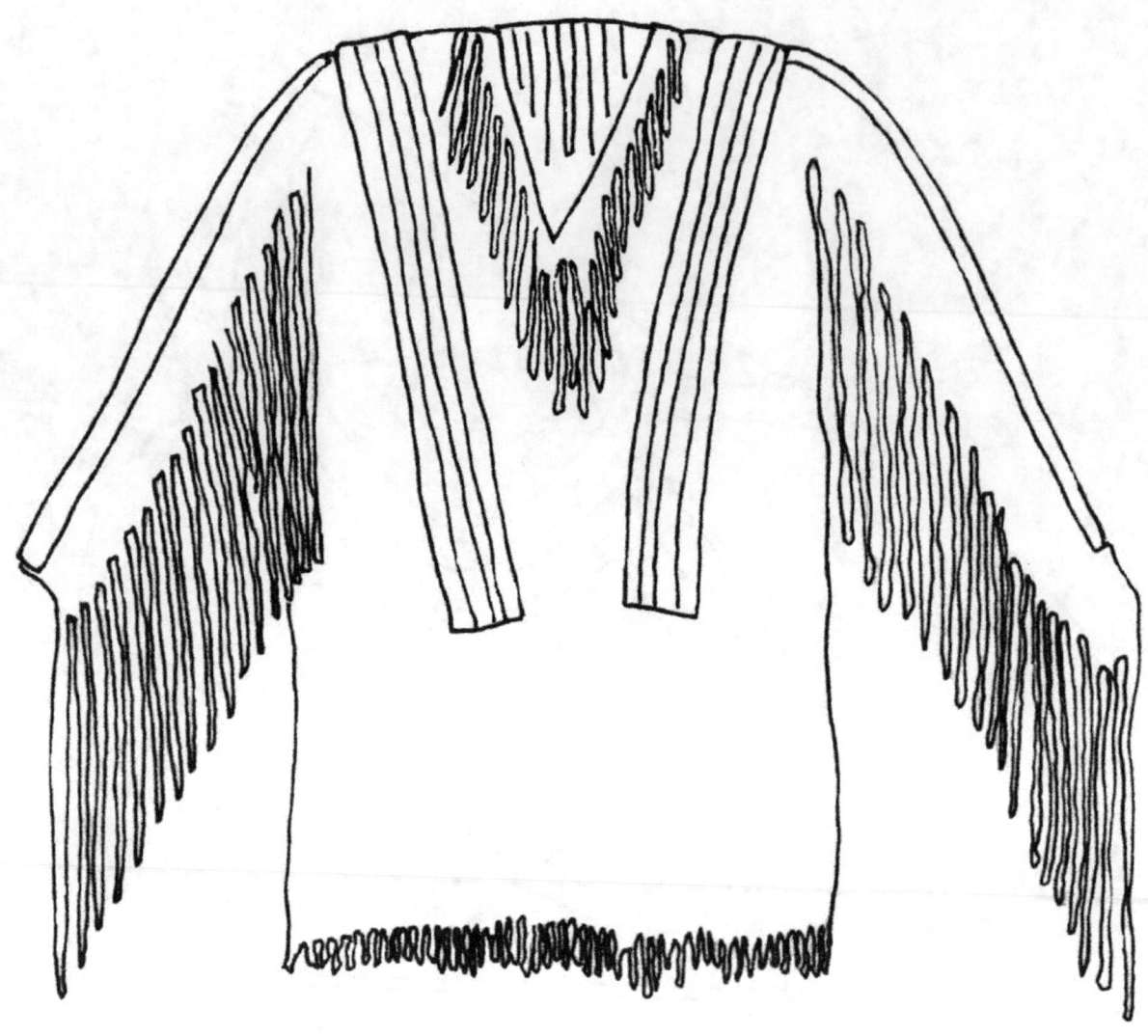

A hide shirt with long fringe and
beadwork strips is a style worn by the
men of many tribes.

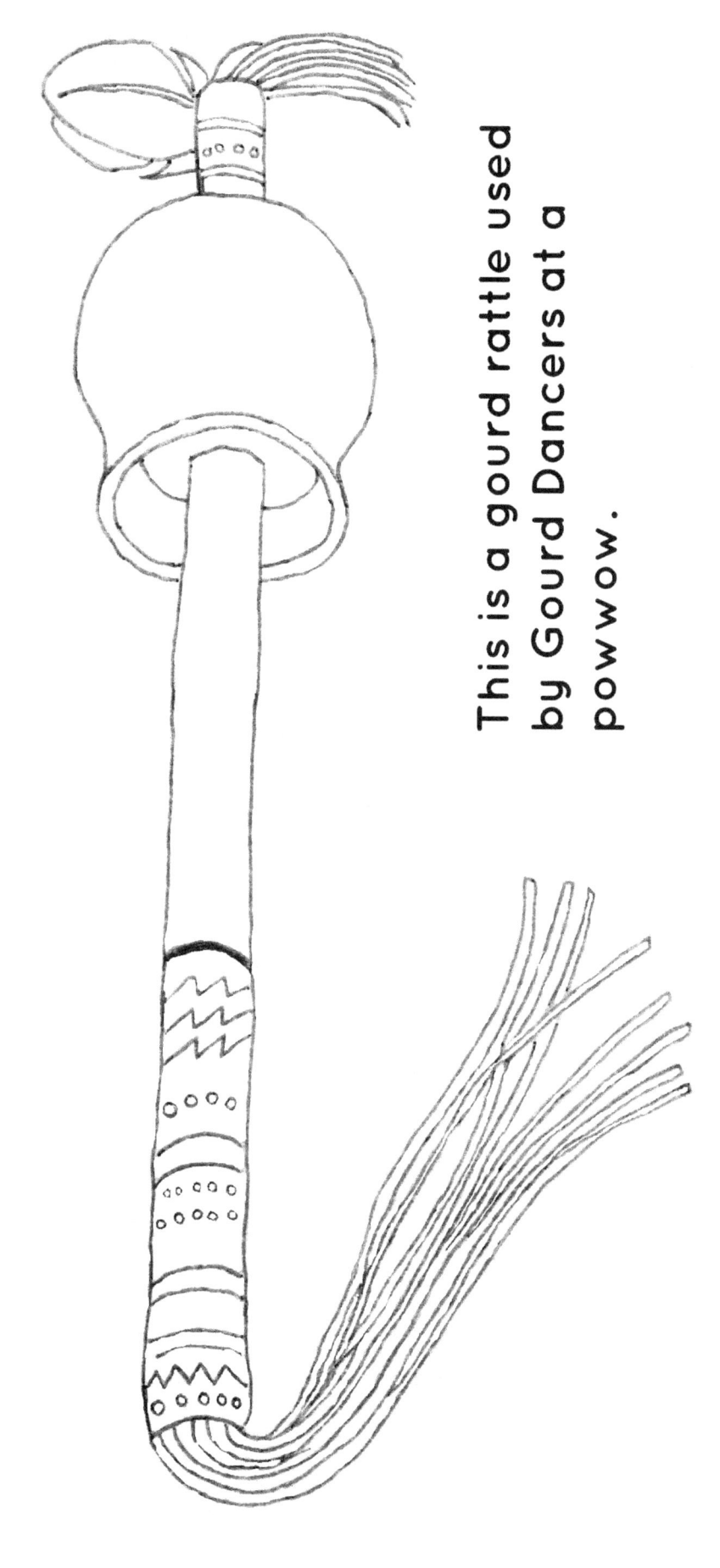

This is a gourd rattle used by Gourd Dancers at a powwow.

The feather
hat, or
Gustoweh, is
a woodland
headdress
worn by the
Mohawk,
Seneca,
Oneida,
Onondaga
and Cayuga

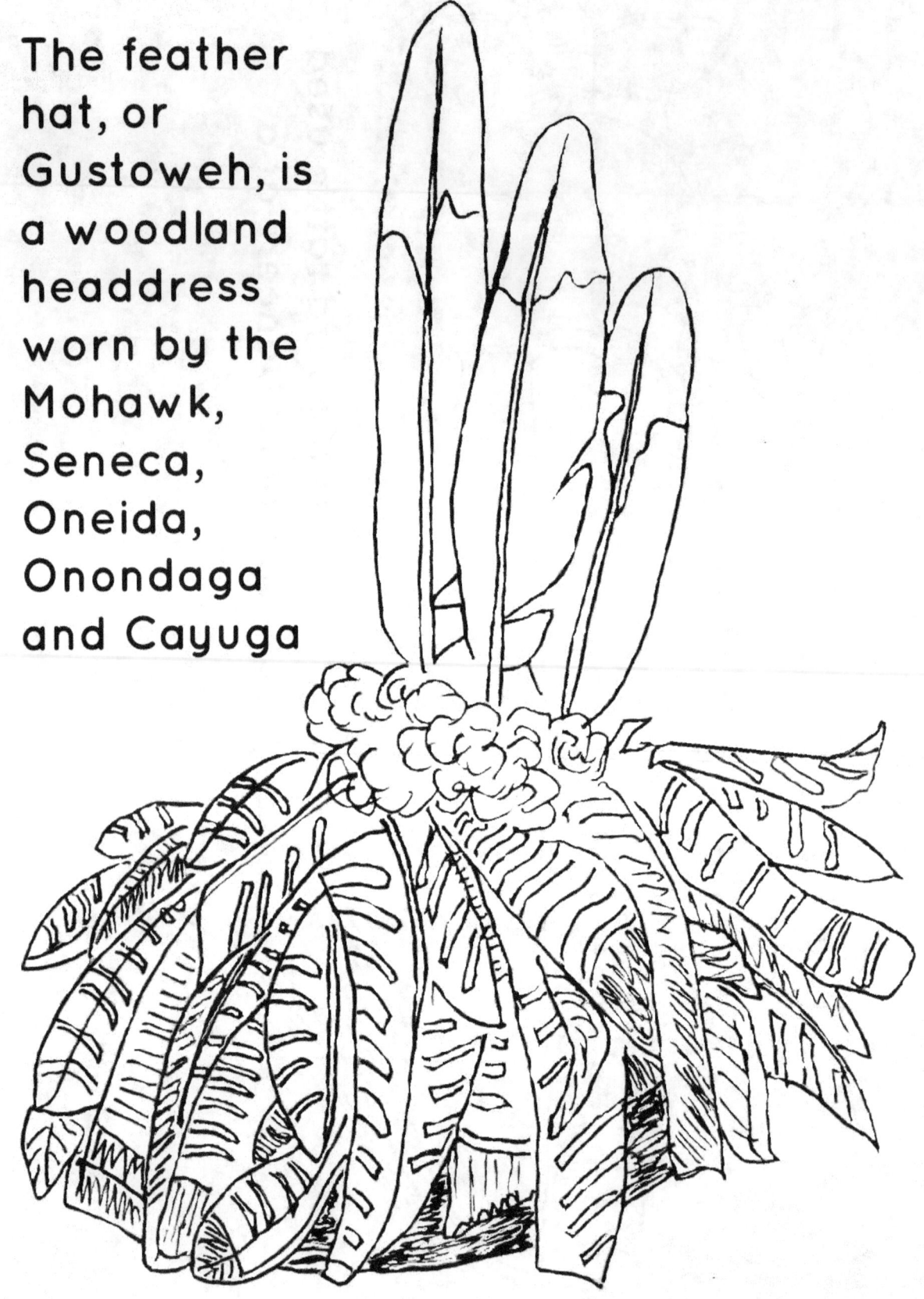

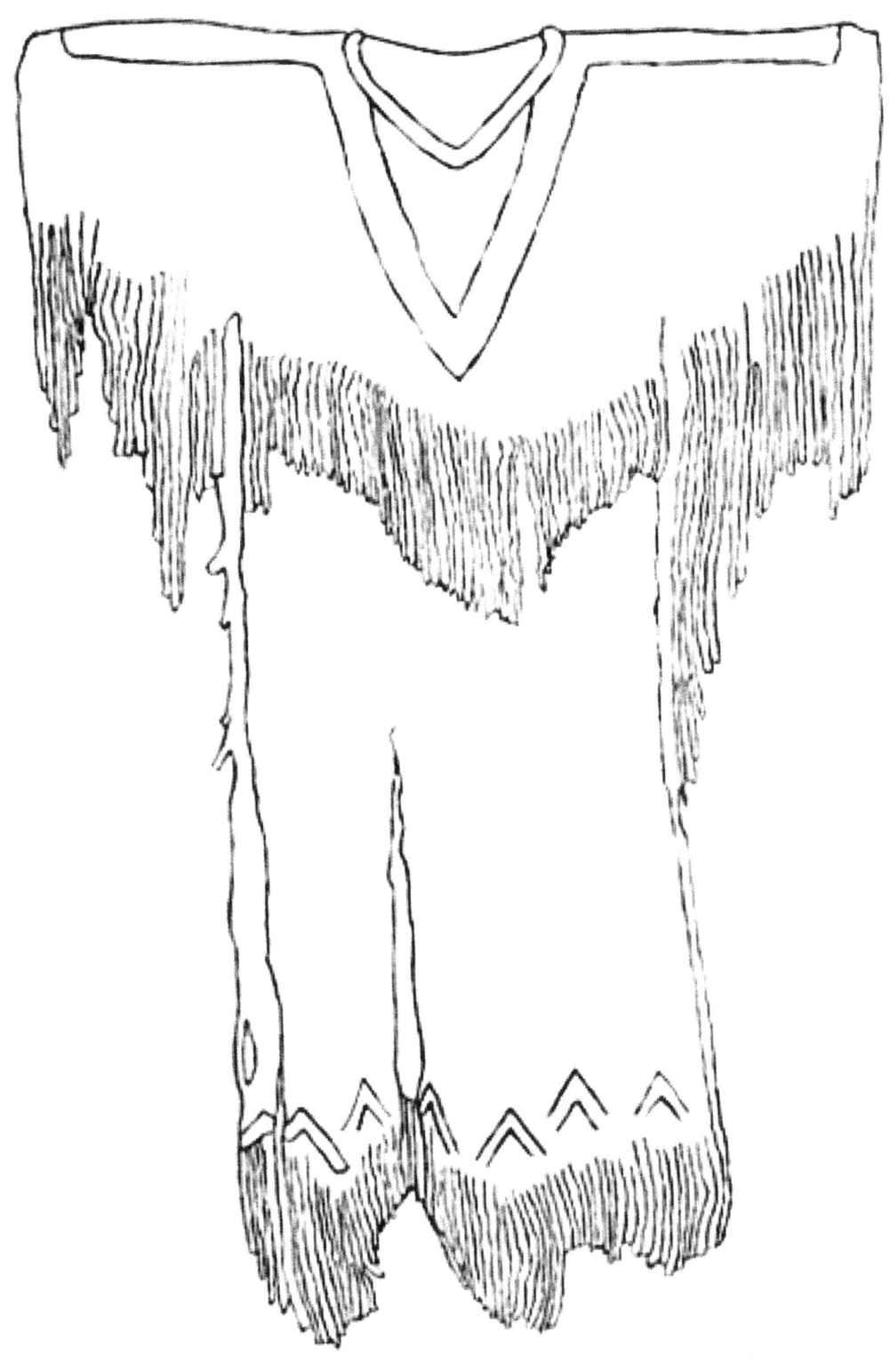

The buckskin dress is a traditional style,
decorated with fringe and beadwork.

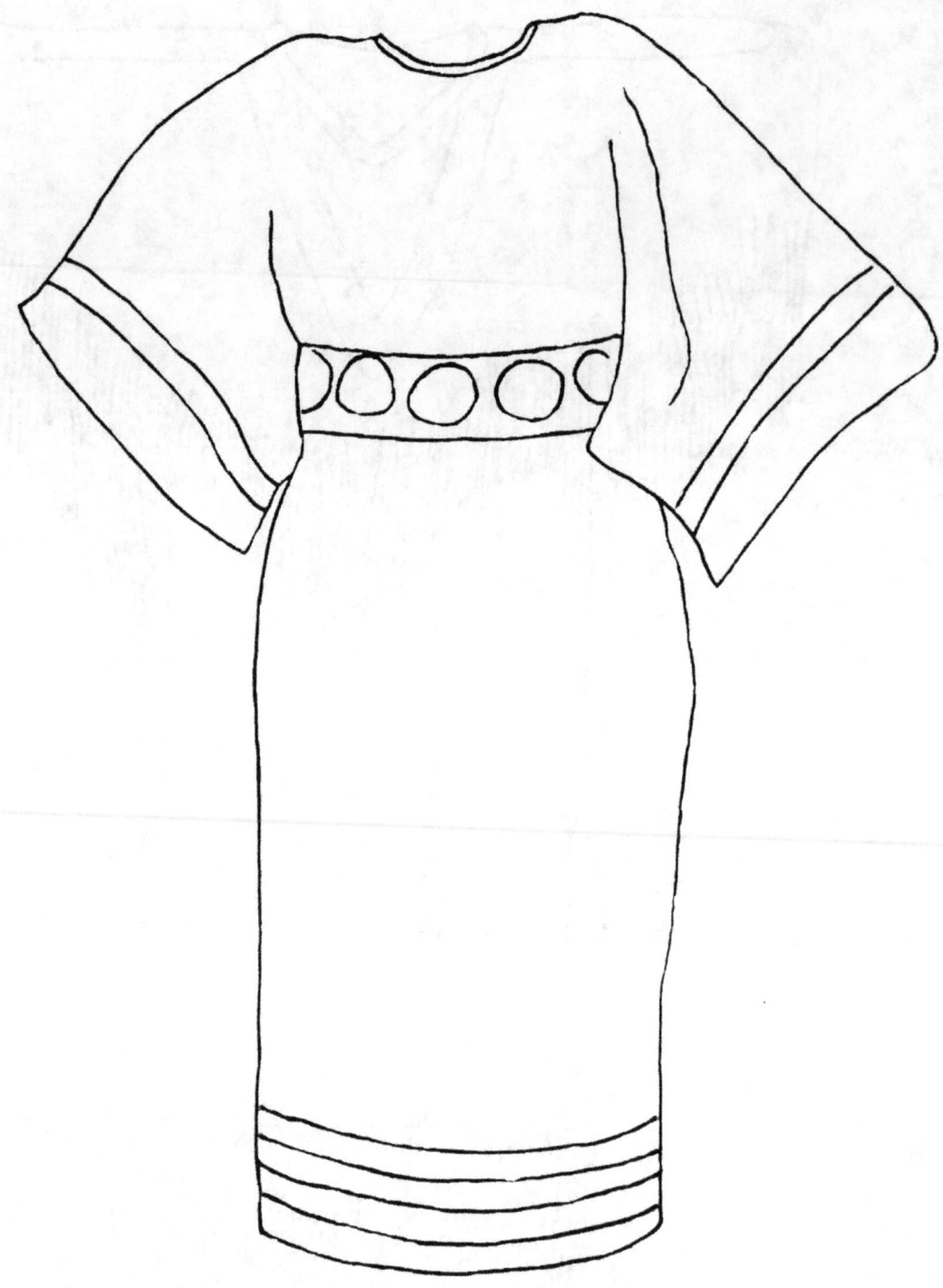

A cloth dress, with colorful trim and a wide leather belt with shiny, brass or silver conchos

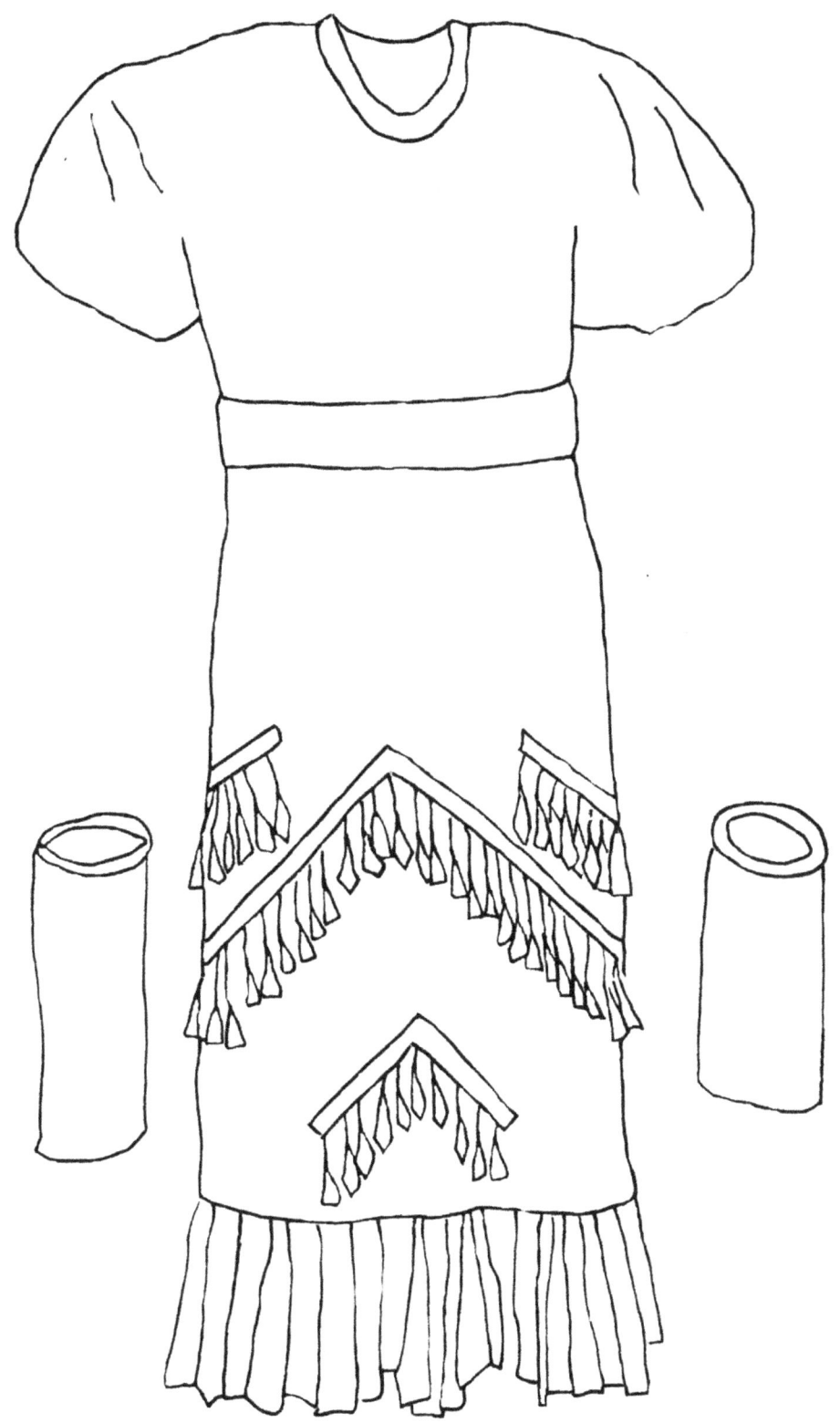

The Jingle dress is a newer style from the Great
Lakes tribes and is a special healing dance.
Decorated with 365 metal cones and bright colors

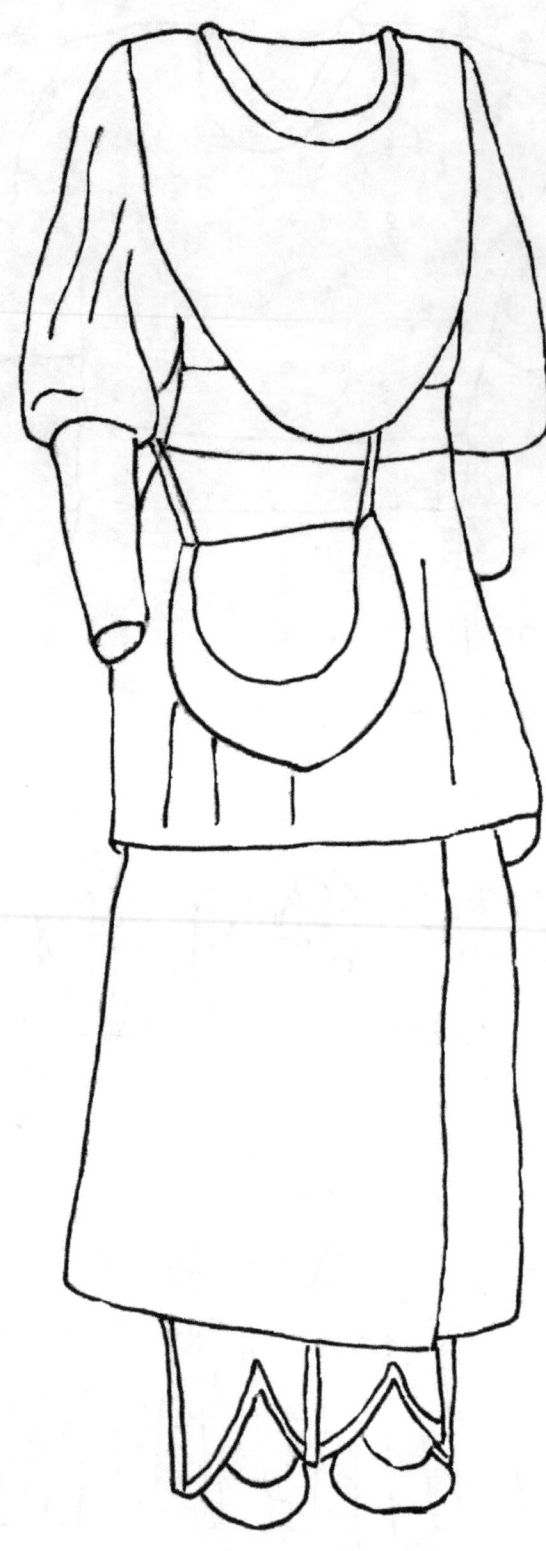

A cloth dress of the Iroquois tribes

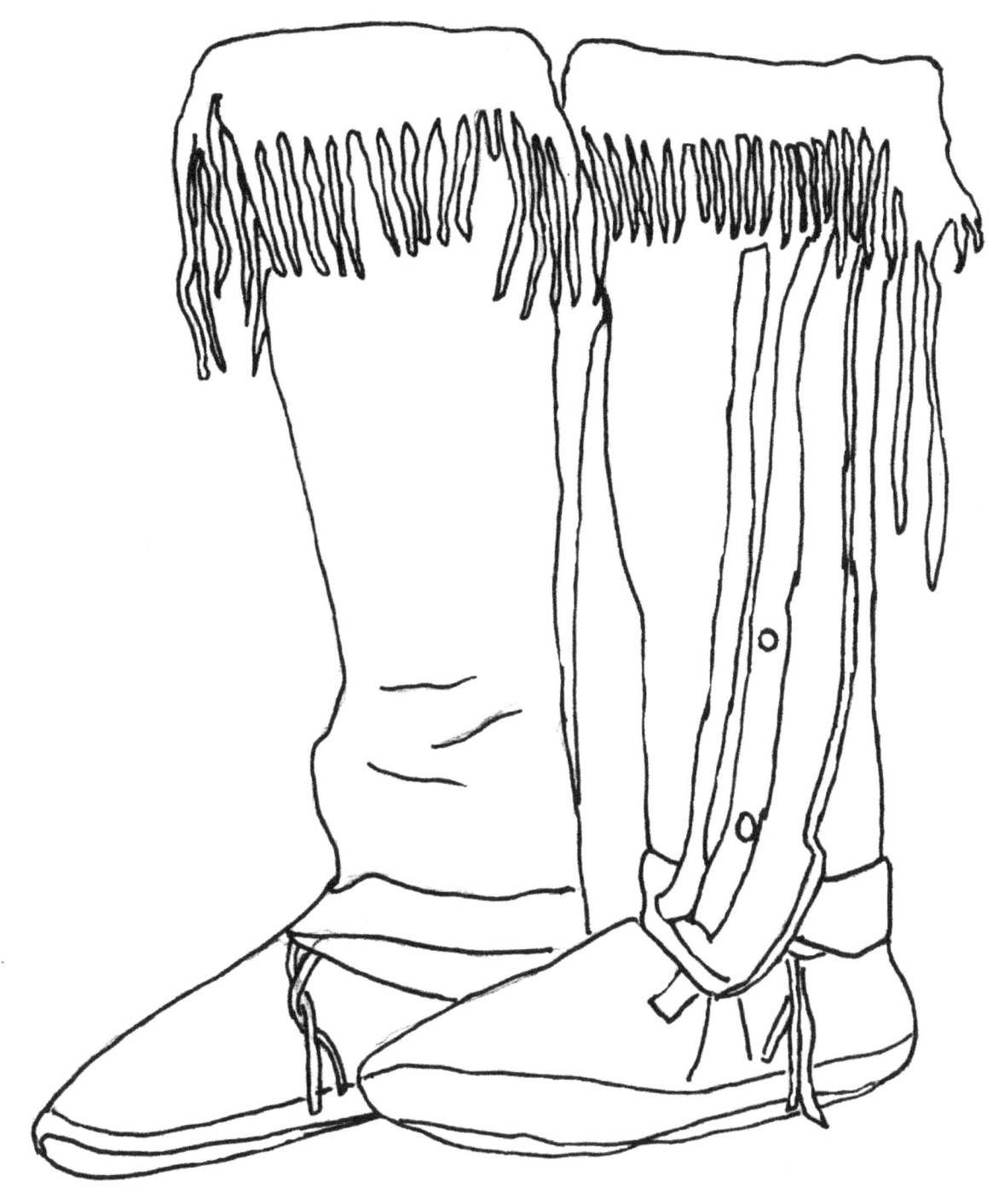

High top moccasins, worn mostly
by the Southwestern peoples,
sometimes beaded.

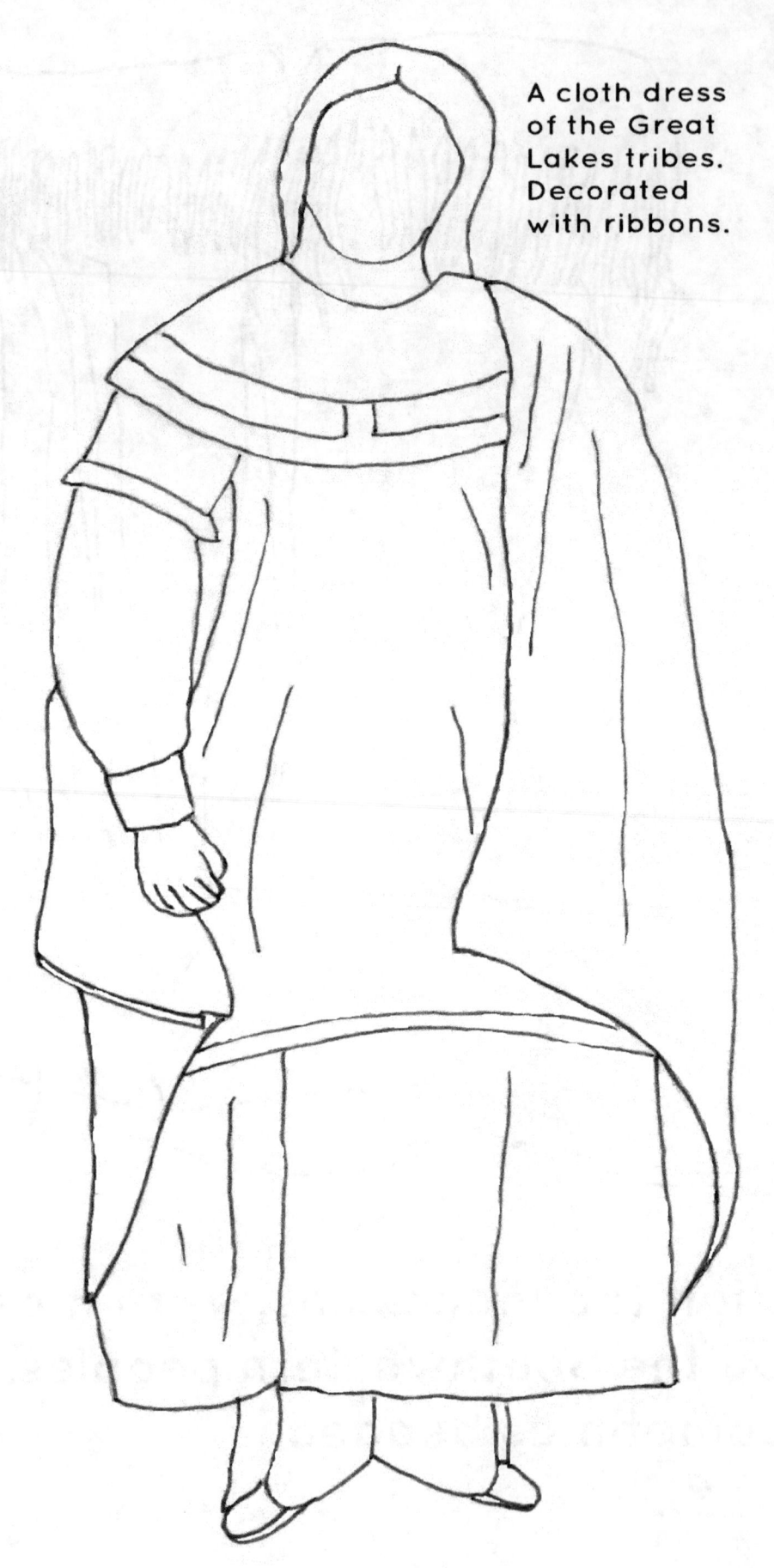

A cloth dress
of the Great
Lakes tribes.
Decorated
with ribbons.

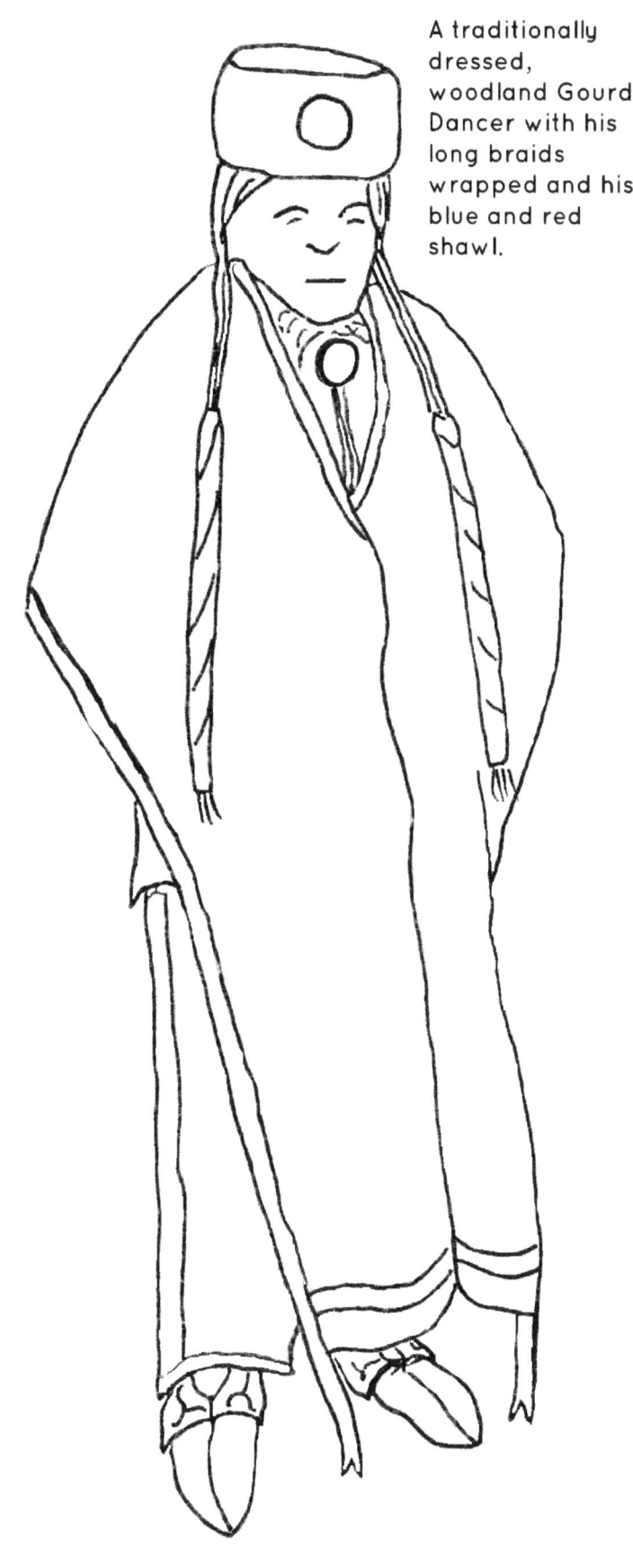

A traditionally dressed, woodland Gourd Dancer with his long braids wrapped and his blue and red shawl.

A Grass dancer and a young lady
dancing the Two-step or Rabbit dance.

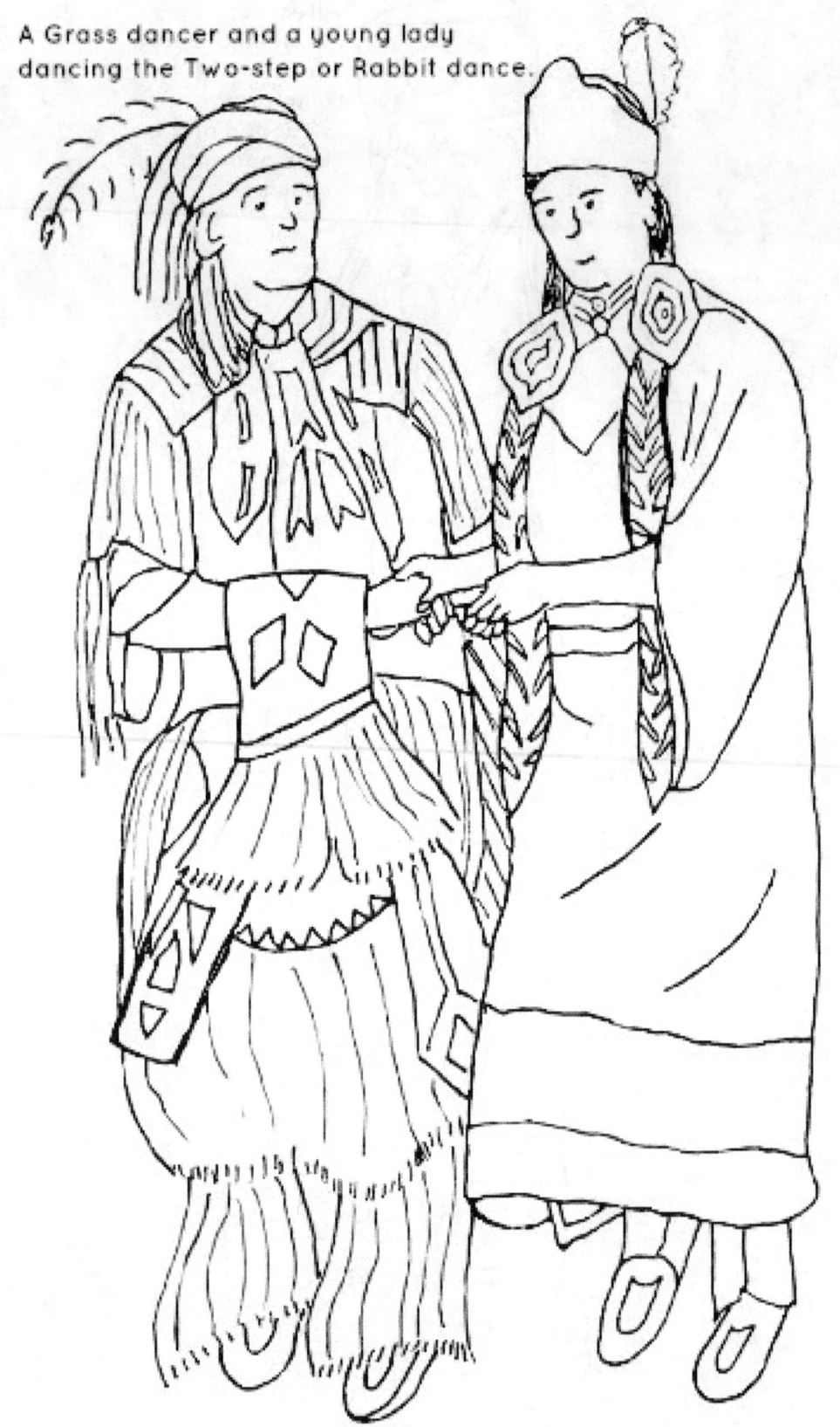

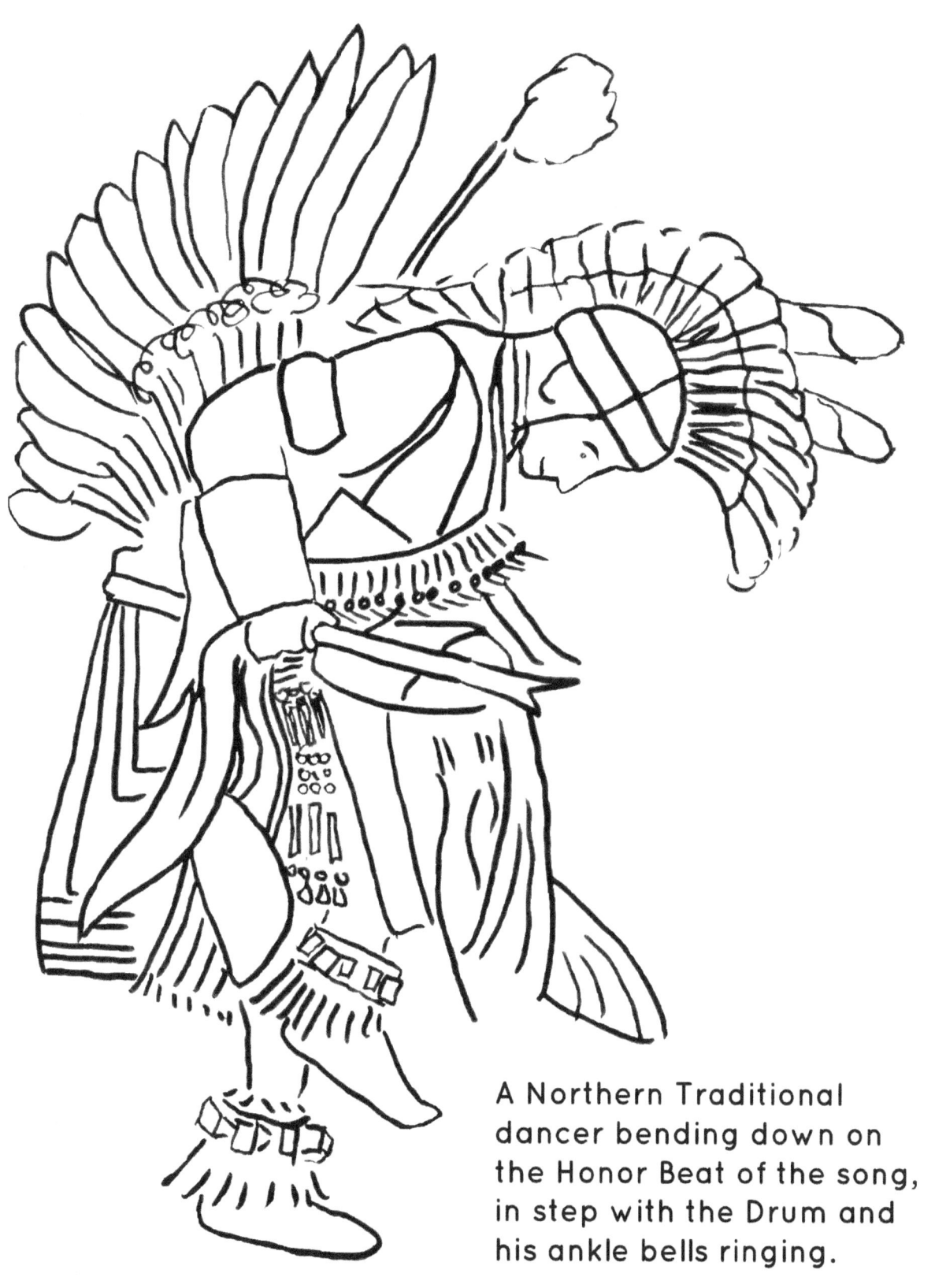

A Northern Traditional
dancer bending down on
the Honor Beat of the song,
in step with the Drum and
his ankle bells ringing.

A fast and flashy
young lady
Shawl dancer

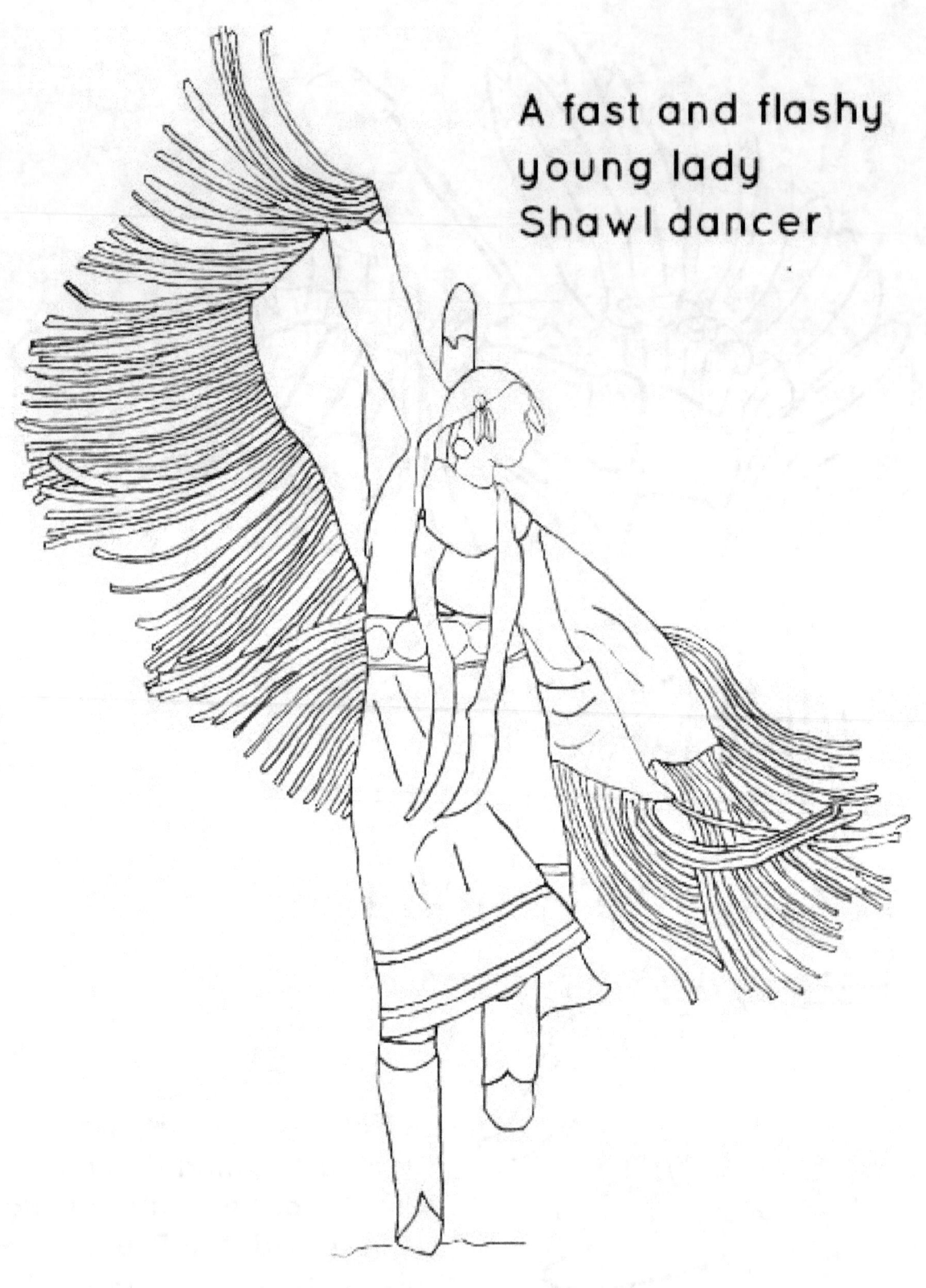

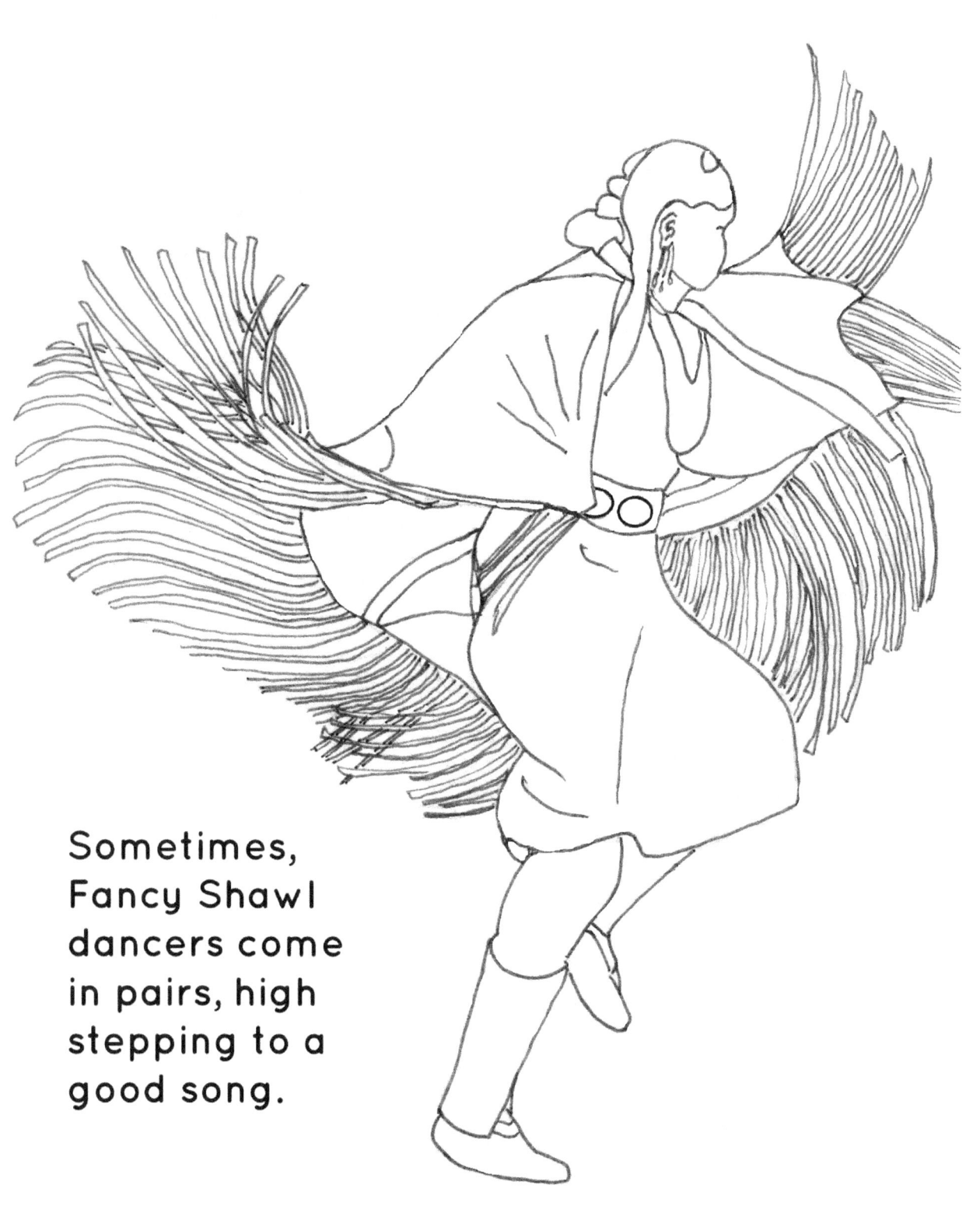

Sometimes,
Fancy Shawl
dancers come
in pairs, high
stepping to a
good song.

As you go around
the arbor you may
find yourself
behind

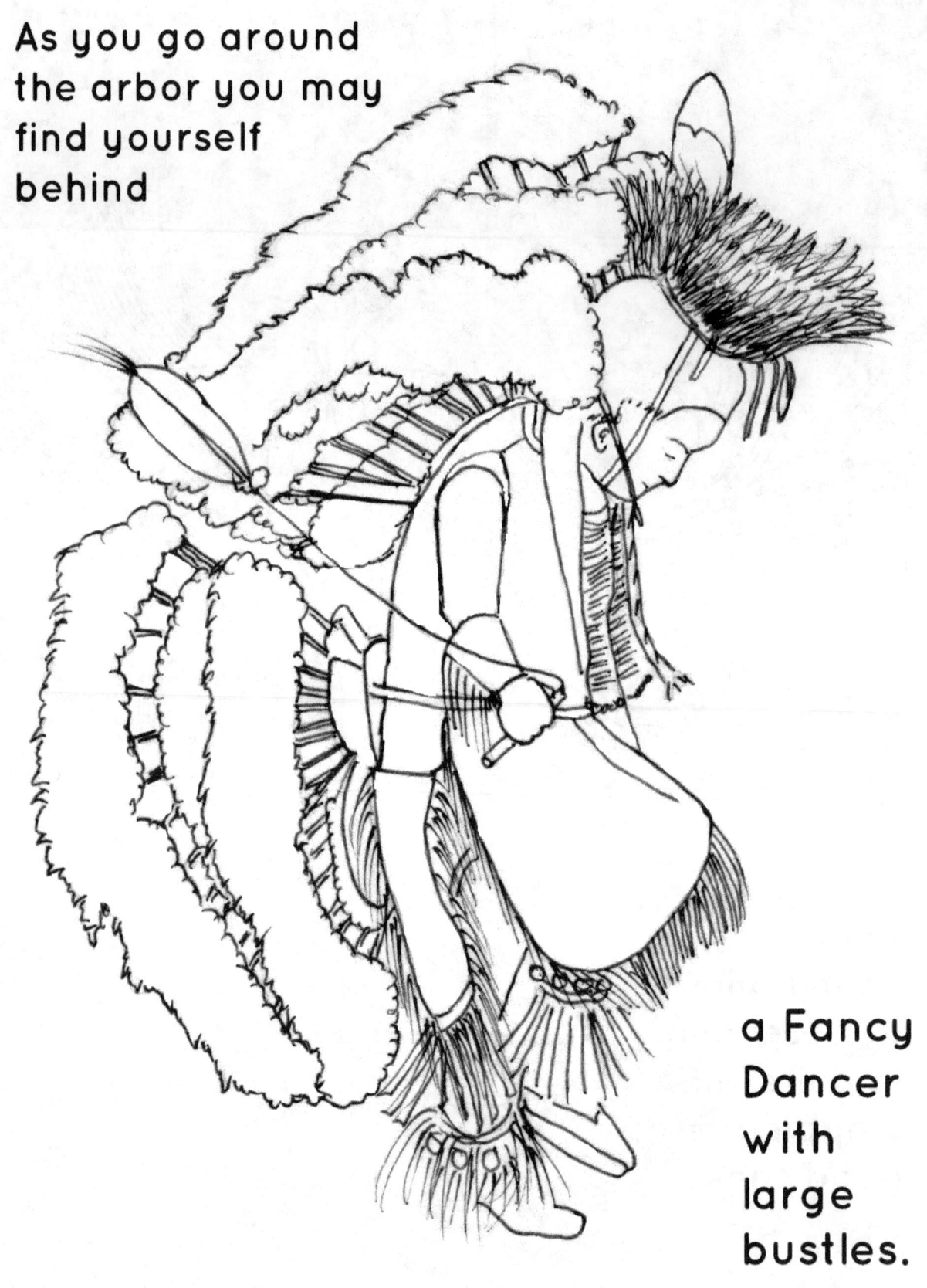

a Fancy
Dancer
with
large
bustles.

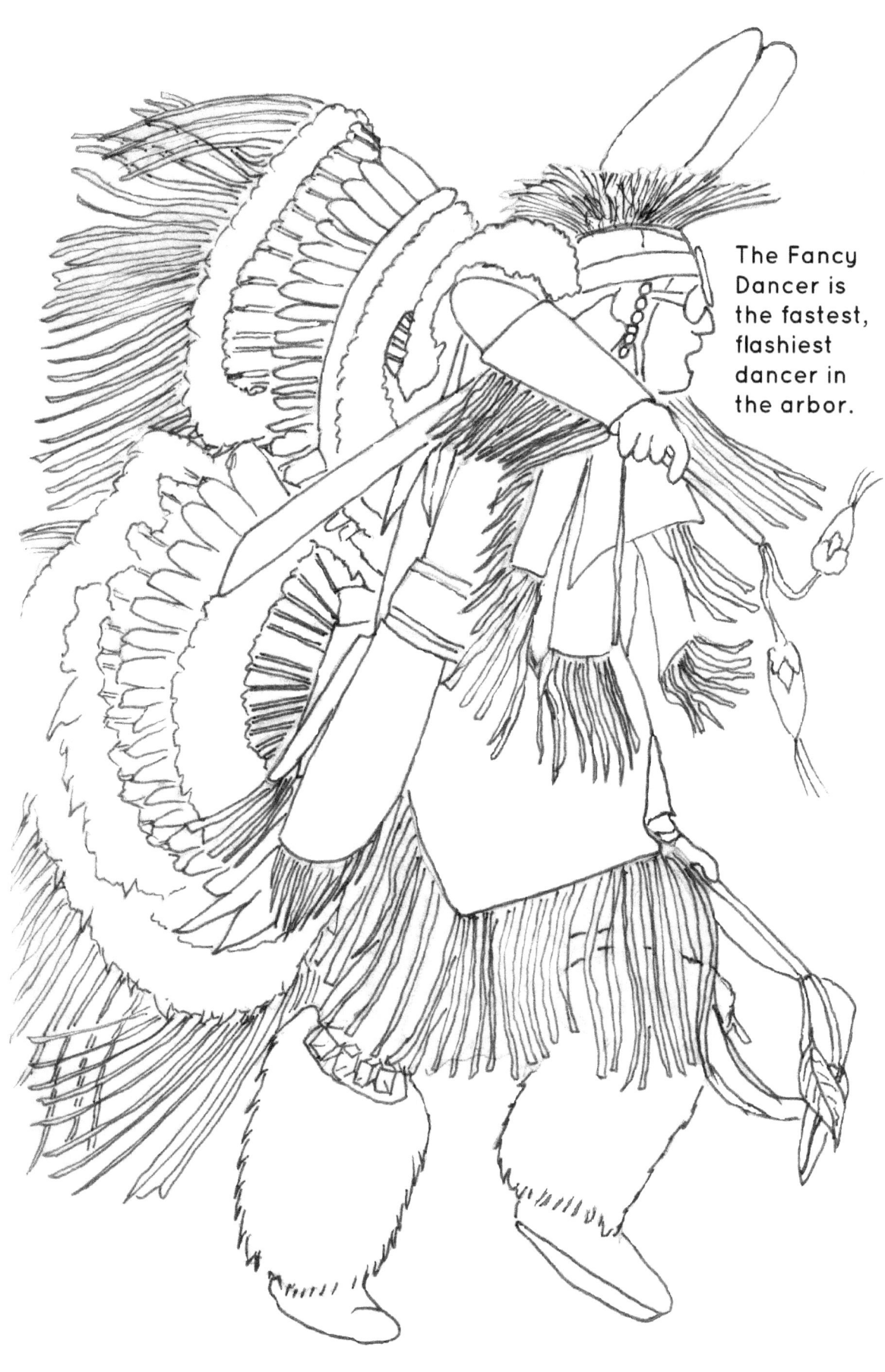

The Fancy Dancer is the fastest, flashiest dancer in the arbor.